In loving memory of
James Howard Davis

Santa Anita Morning Rhapsody

Karen S. Davis

Tributes

Santa Anita is a place all its own, and these photos show that. They're unbelievable!
   —***Paul Atkinson***, Jockey

These beautiful photographs reveal the truly unique experience of a Santa Anita Park sunrise. Watching the elegant yet powerful thoroughbreds against the backdrop of the San Gabriel Mountains is awe-inspiring. Any horsemen will tell you this is their favorite time of day. It's a memorable experience not soon forgotten, and the perfect way to start the upcoming race day.
   —***George Haines***, General Manager, Santa Anita Park

Karen has taken stunning photos. Santa Anita is lucky to have her.
   —***Ron McAnally***, Eclipse Award-winning Trainer

At Santa Anita, as the sun rises in the morning and the San Gabriel Mountains come into view, there's not a more beautiful setting in which to see the powerful thoroughbreds. This was my first thought when I viewed these lovely photos and remembered the mornings when I used to work horses. Karen's photographs are just great.
   —***Laffit Pincay, Jr.***, National Thoroughbred Racing Hall of Fame Jockey
      Eclipse Award; George Woolf Memorial Jockey Award

These pictures describe the real beauty of morning and animal ... remembrances of time well spent at Santa Anita. Thanks, Karen!
   —***Gino Roncelli***, Member, Board of Directors of Los Angeles Turf Club

These pictures are really pretty ... Santa Anita has always been such a beautiful track.
   —***Ron Turcotte***, National Thoroughbred Racing Hall of Fame Jockey
      George Woolf Memorial Jockey Award; Triple Crown winner on Secretariat, 1973

These incredible photos capture all the best moments of the morning. The sound of the hooves ... the sound of their breath ... morning chills that lead to afternoon thrills. It's like watching the racing community come alive.
   —***Patrick Valenzuela***, Jockey

Beautiful photographs! Everybody's going to want this book!
   —***Jack Van Berg***, National Thoroughbred Racing Hall of Fame Trainer

These are damn good photos ... the next best thing to being there!
   —***Ray York***, Jockey, Kentucky Derby winner on Determine, 1954

Every morning here is like a snowflake. Santa Anita is a gorgeous place and these photographs capture it beautifully. They're amazing!
   —***Howard Zucker***, Trainer

Preface

Morning at Santa Anita racetrack is like no other time or place on earth. The average racing enthusiast enjoys the afternoon fanfare of racing, but never sees the way of life that begins well before dawn and continues three hundred sixty-five days of the year, year in and year out. Routine and dangerous at the same time, it's as unpredictable and beautiful as the horses themselves and the changing sunrises over the San Gabriel Mountains. All of the moments that define the morning at Santa Anita are captured in the stunning photography of this book. Even those of us who've spent a good deal of our lives here can forget how lucky we are. Karen is here to remind us— and encourage us to look around with new appreciation. But I'm a rider, not a writer. Let the pictures, truly worth a thousand words, speak for themselves.

Eddie Delahoussaye
NATIONAL THOROUGHBRED RACING HALL OF FAME JOCKEY

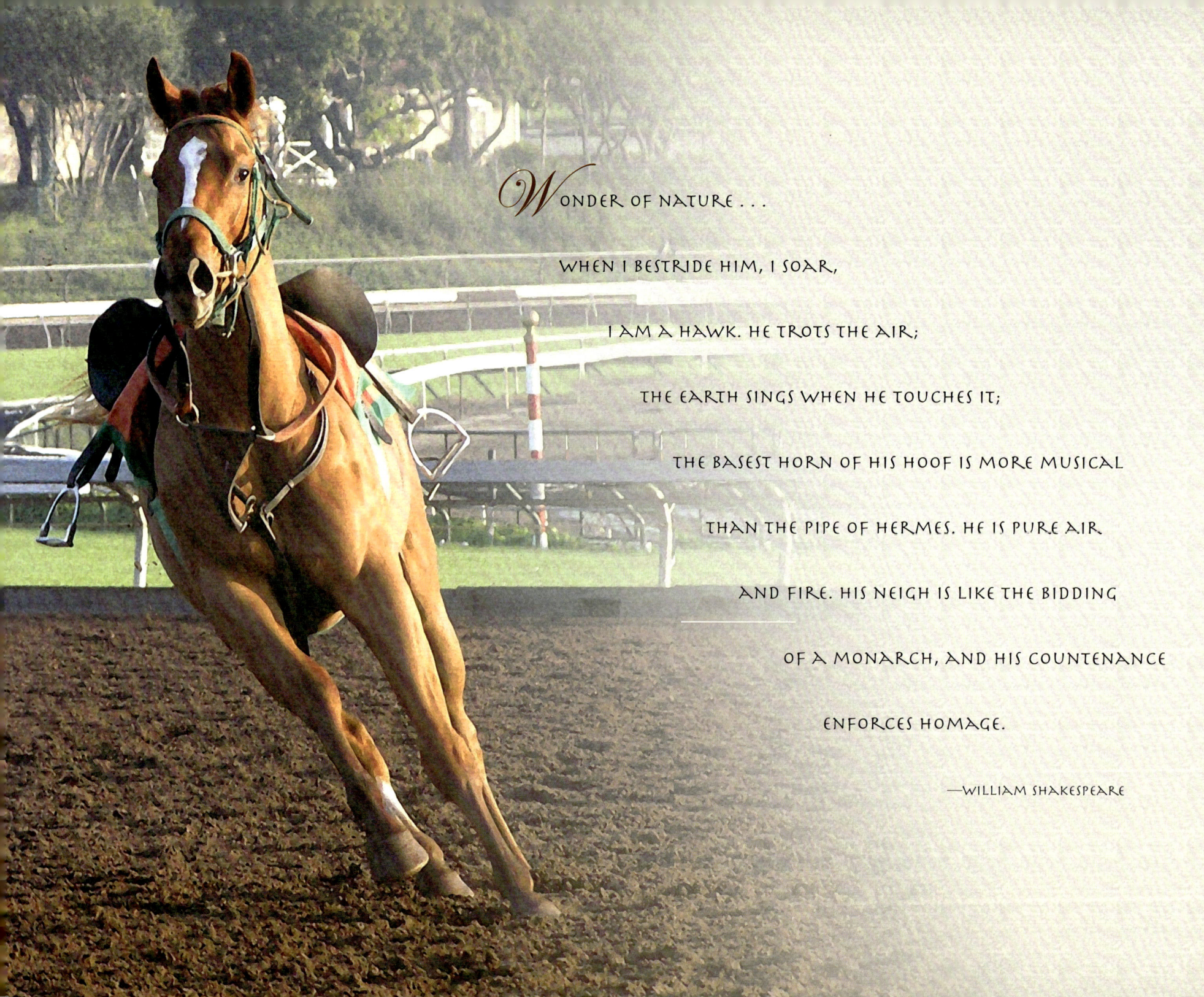

Wonder of nature...

When I bestride him, I soar,

I am a hawk. He trots the air;

The earth sings when he touches it;

The basest horn of his hoof is more musical

than the pipe of Hermes. He is pure air

and fire. His neigh is like the bidding

of a monarch, and his countenance

enforces homage.

—William Shakespeare

Introduction

by Richard Mandella
NATIONAL THOROUGHBRED RACING HALL OF FAME TRAINER

Karen Davis has done a magnificent job of capturing the scenes of morning training hours—in most horsemen's minds, the greatest part of the day. Most people who enjoy racing don't realize how special these early hours are, watching the ins and outs of training and the relationship between horse and man.

If you look closely at the horses' expressions in these photos, you can imagine every emotion from fear to sheer joy, and everything in between. Karen has been able to capture these feelings through her passion for the horse and her dedication to this project.

I am very proud to be able to introduce her collection, and suggest that it would be a great addition to anyone's library.

STEED THREATENS STEED, IN HIGH AND BOASTFUL NEIGHS—PIERCING THE NIGHT'S DULL EAR . . .

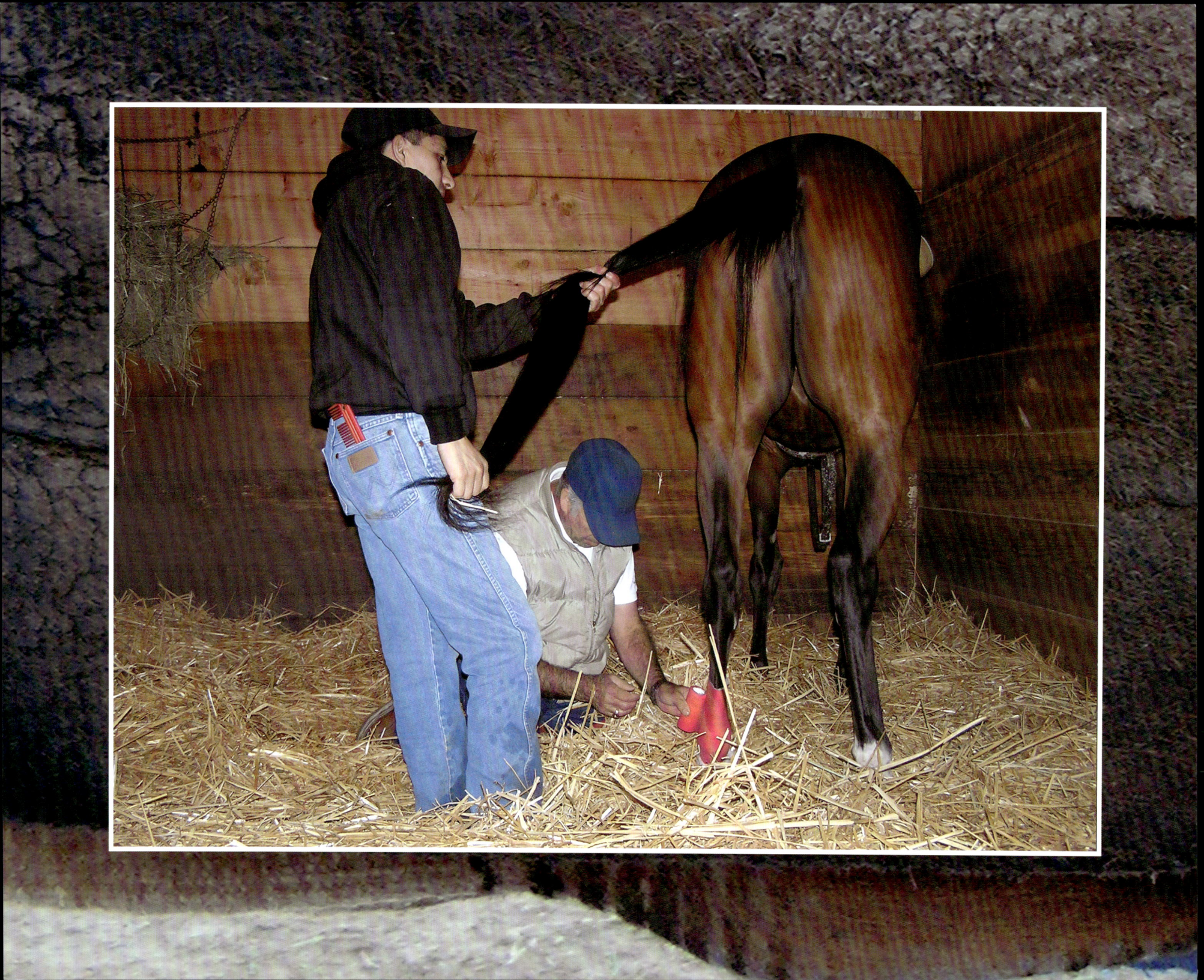

HOW WENT HE UNDER HIM? SO PROUDLY AS IF HE DISDAIN'D THE GROUND.

FOR THROUGH HIS MANE AND TAIL THE HIGH WIND SINGS,
FANNING HAIRS, WHO WAVE LIKE FEATHER'D WINGS.

IMPERIOUSLY HE LEAPS, HE NEIGHS, HE BOUNDS,
AND NOW HIS WOVEN GIRTHS HE BREAKS ASUNDER . . .

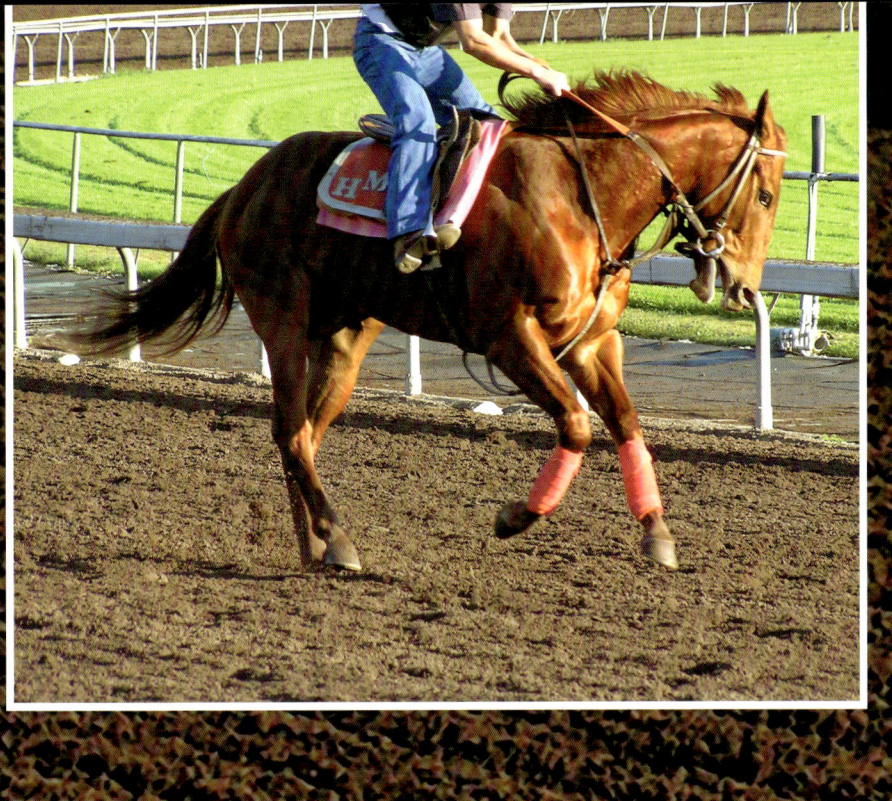

GALLOP APACE, YOU FIERY-FOOTED STEEDS . . .

O! FOR A HORSE WITH WINGS!

THE BEARING EARTH WITH HIS HARD HOOF HE WOUNDS,
WHOSE HOLLOW WOMB RESOUNDS LIKE HEAVEN'S THUNDER . . .

His ears up-prick'd; his braided hanging mane
Upon his compass'd crest now stand on end;
His nostrils drink the air, and forth again,
As from a furnace, vapours doth he send;
His eye, which scornfully glisters like fire,
Shows his hot courage and his high desire.

SOMETIMES HE TROTS, AS IF HE TOLD THE STEPS,
WITH GENTLE MAJESTY AND MODEST PRIDE ...

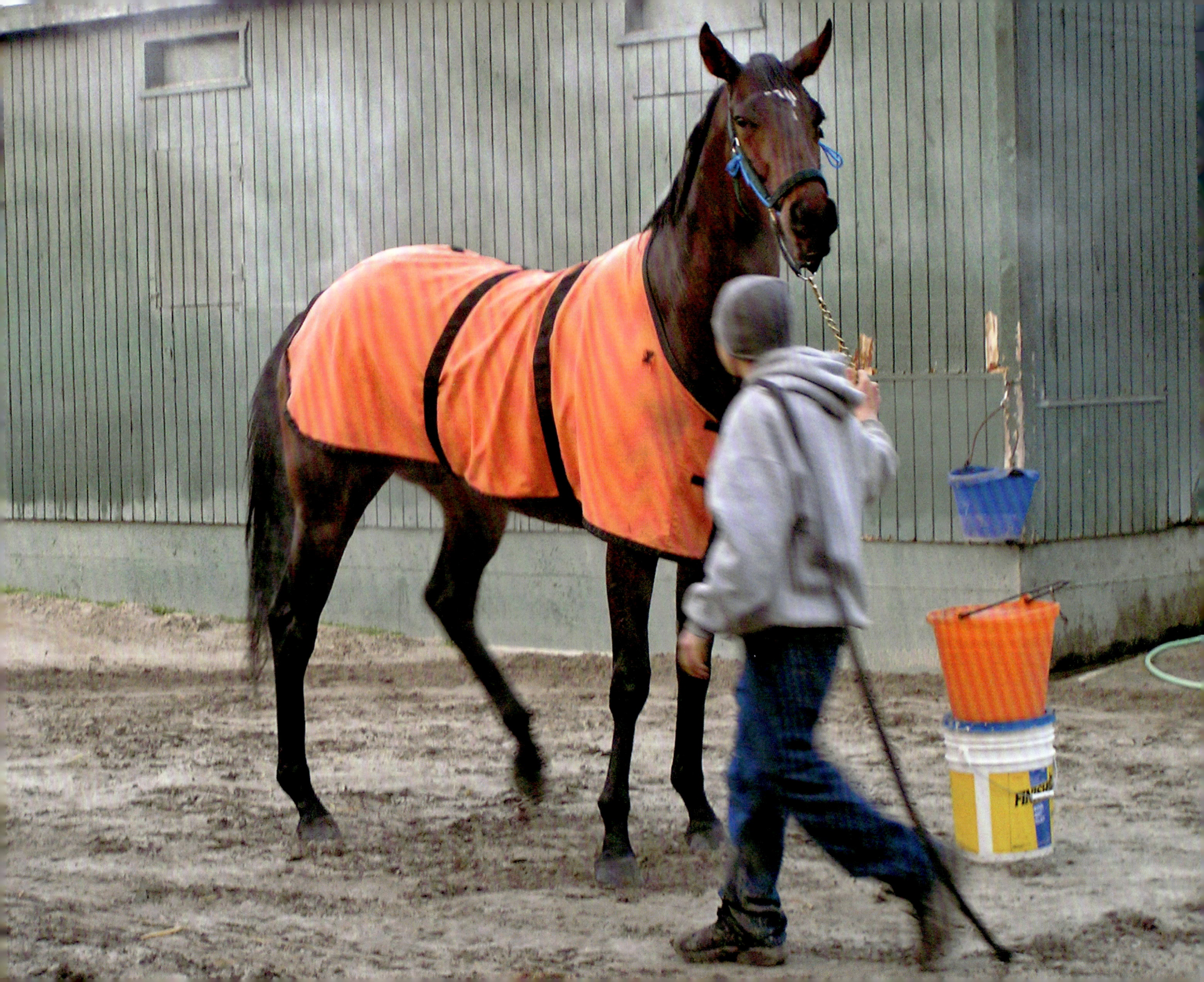

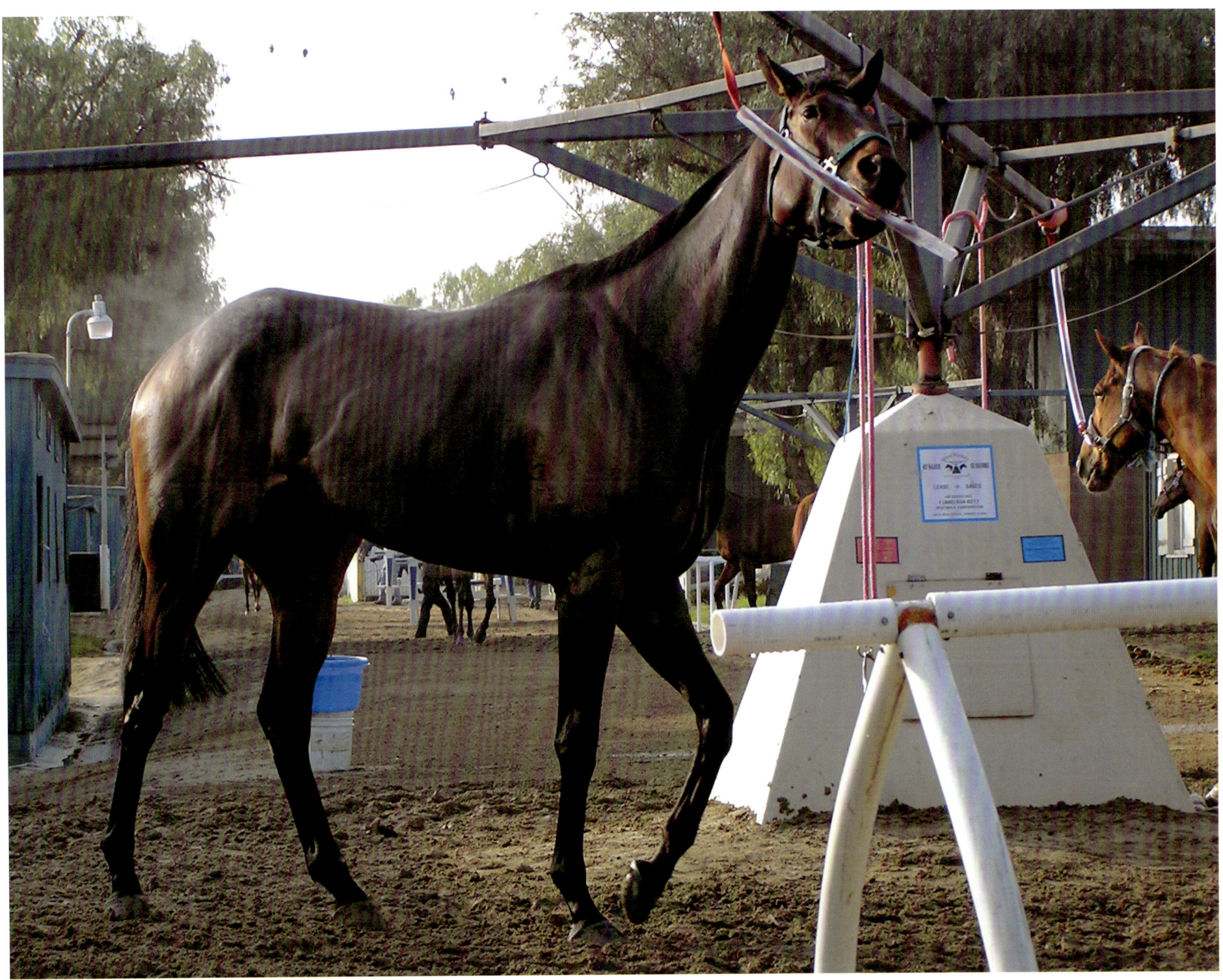

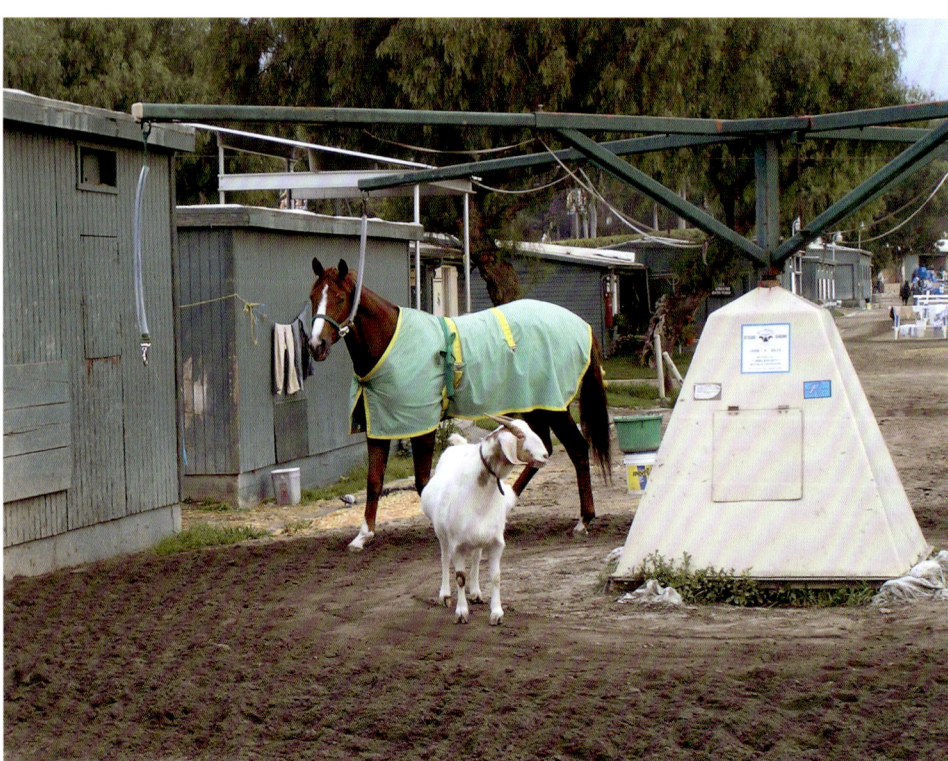

HEELS MAY KICK AT HEAVEN...

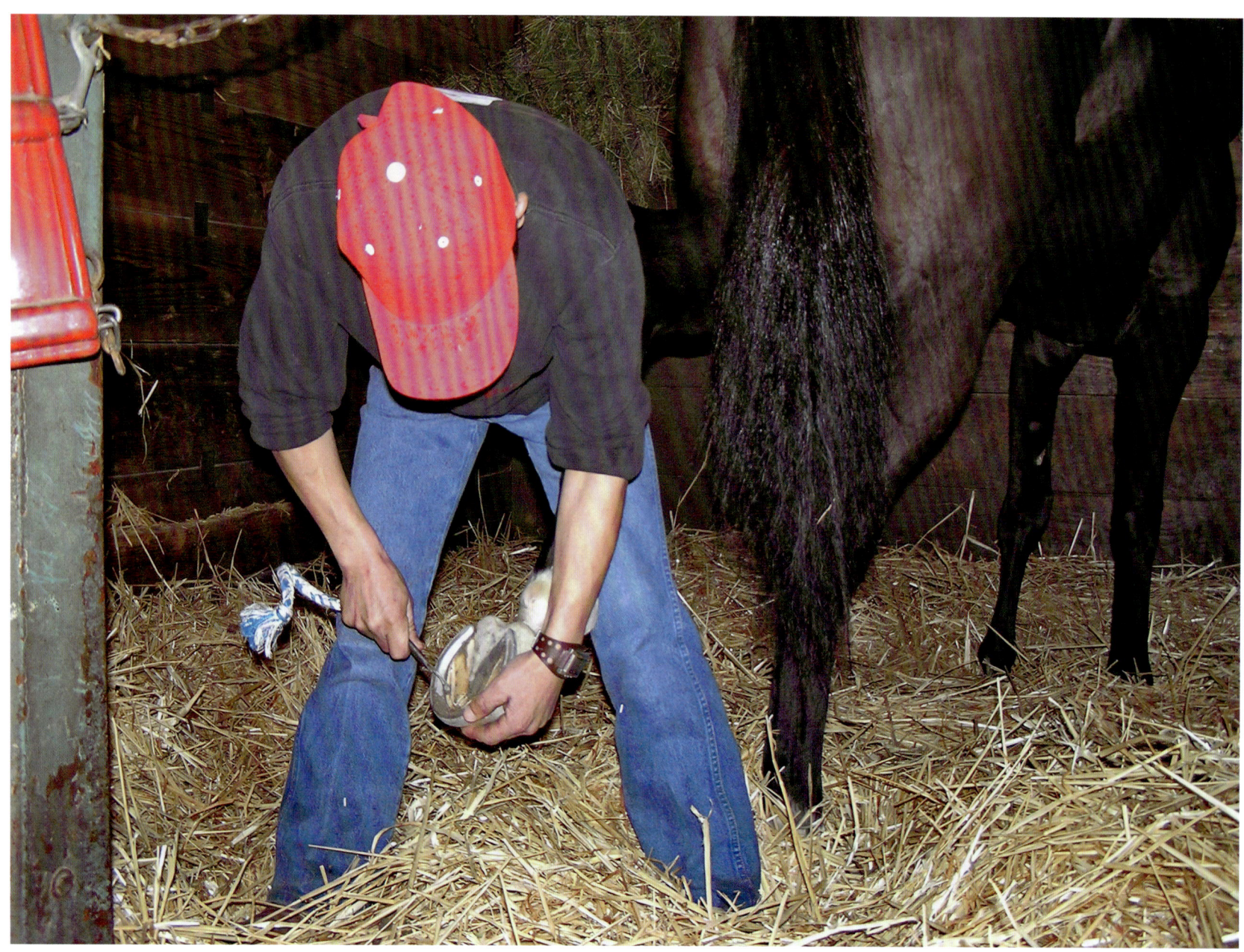

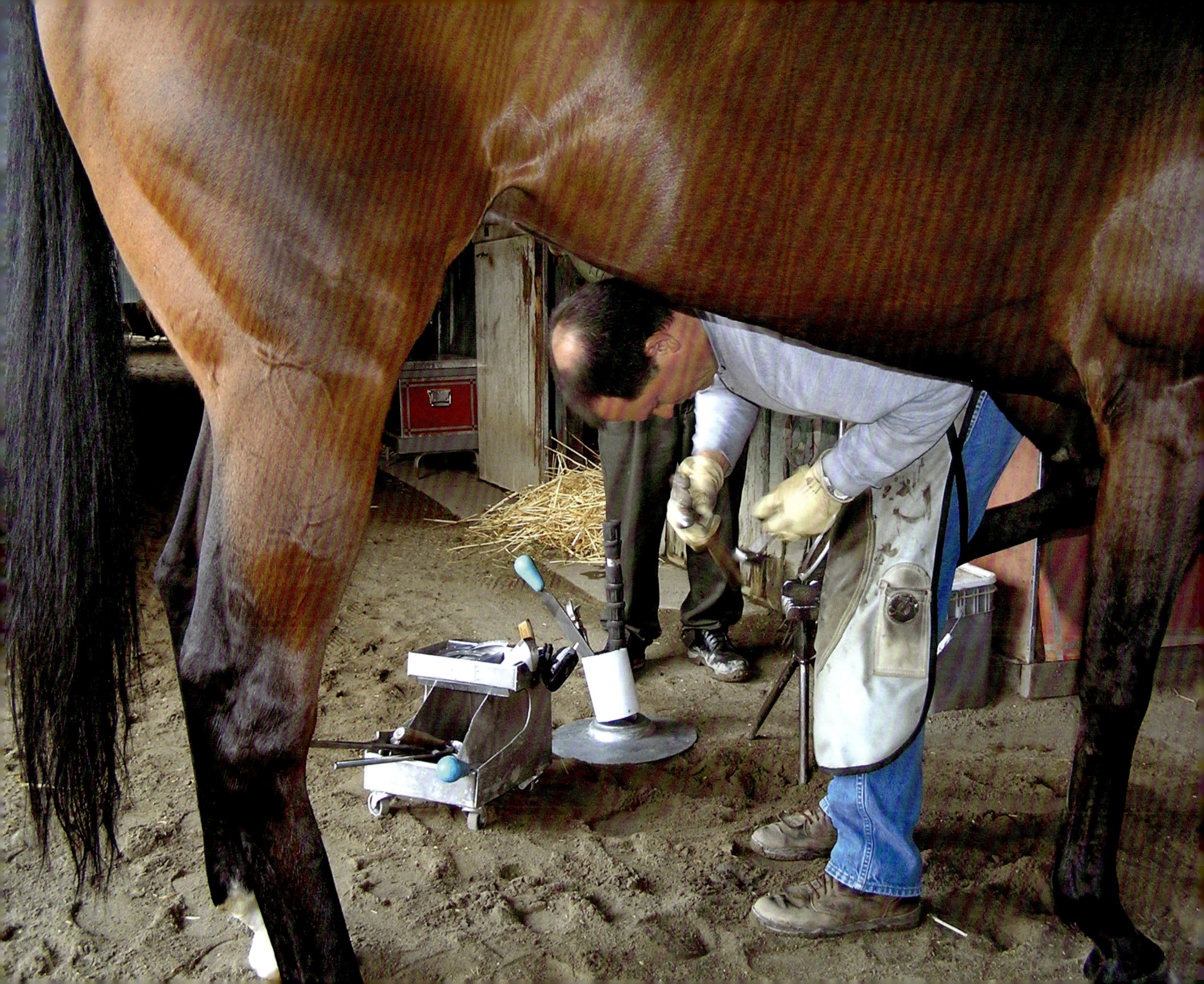

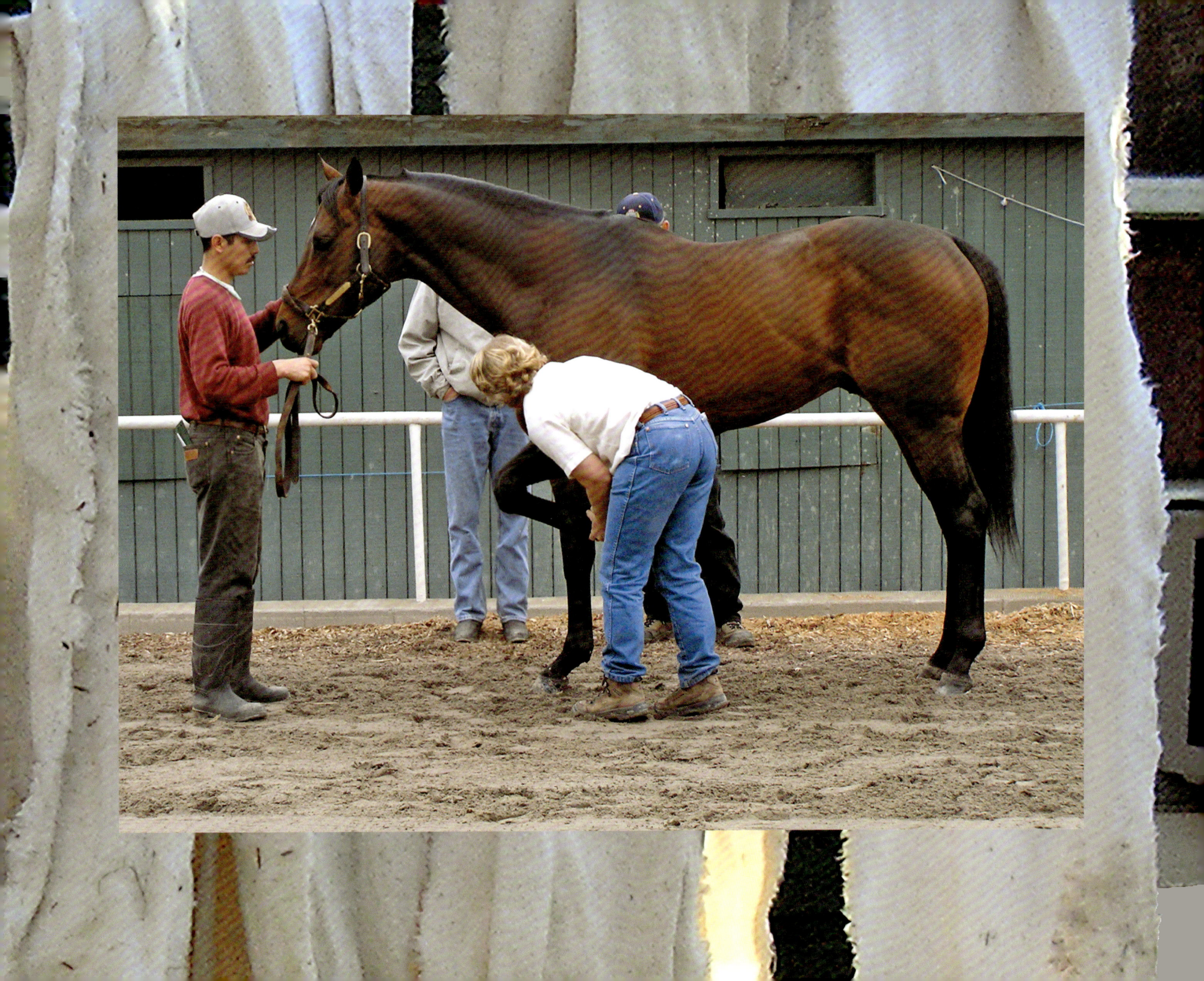

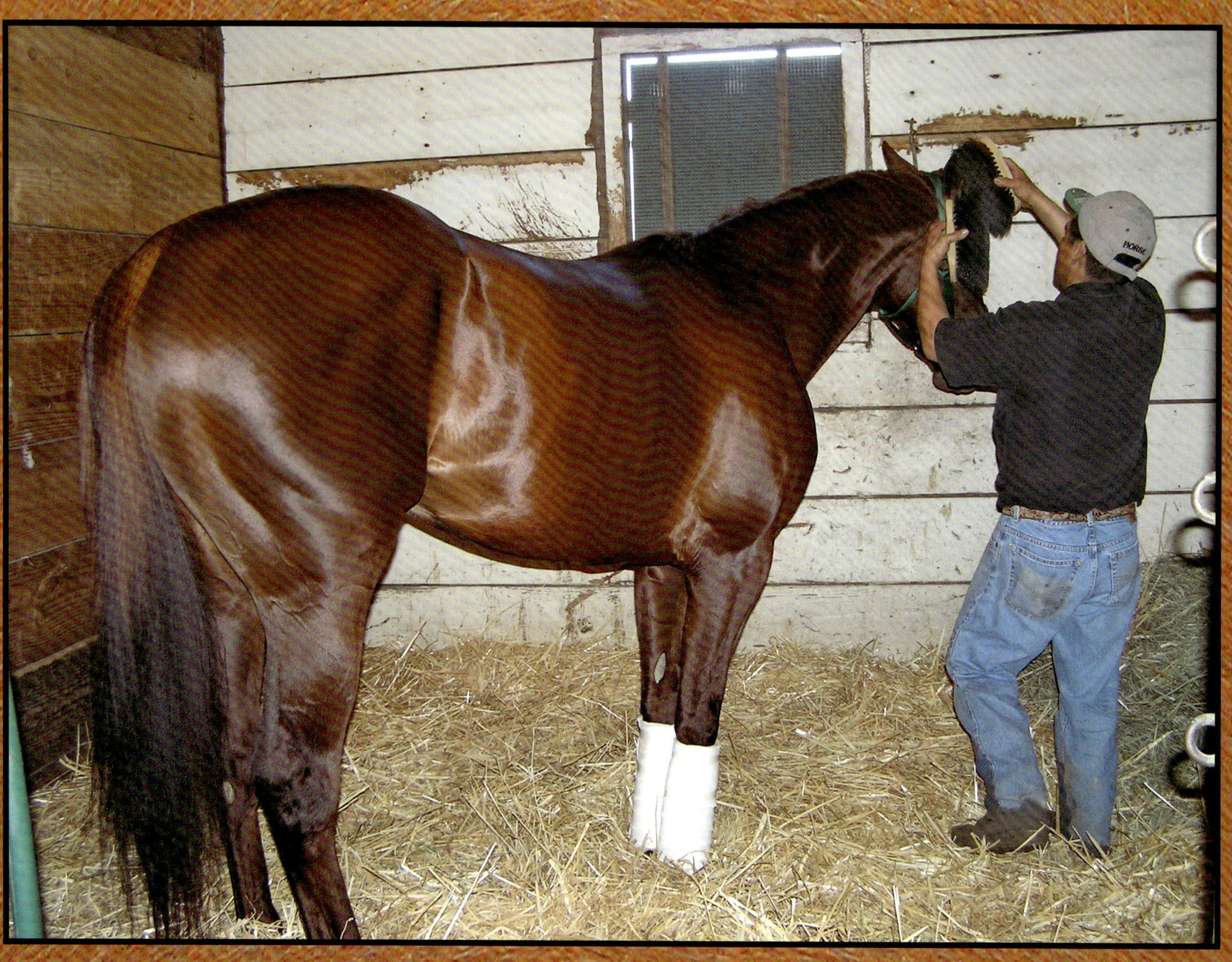

IF SHE BE UP, I'LL SPEAK WITH HER;

IF NOT, LET HER LIE STILL, AND DREAM.

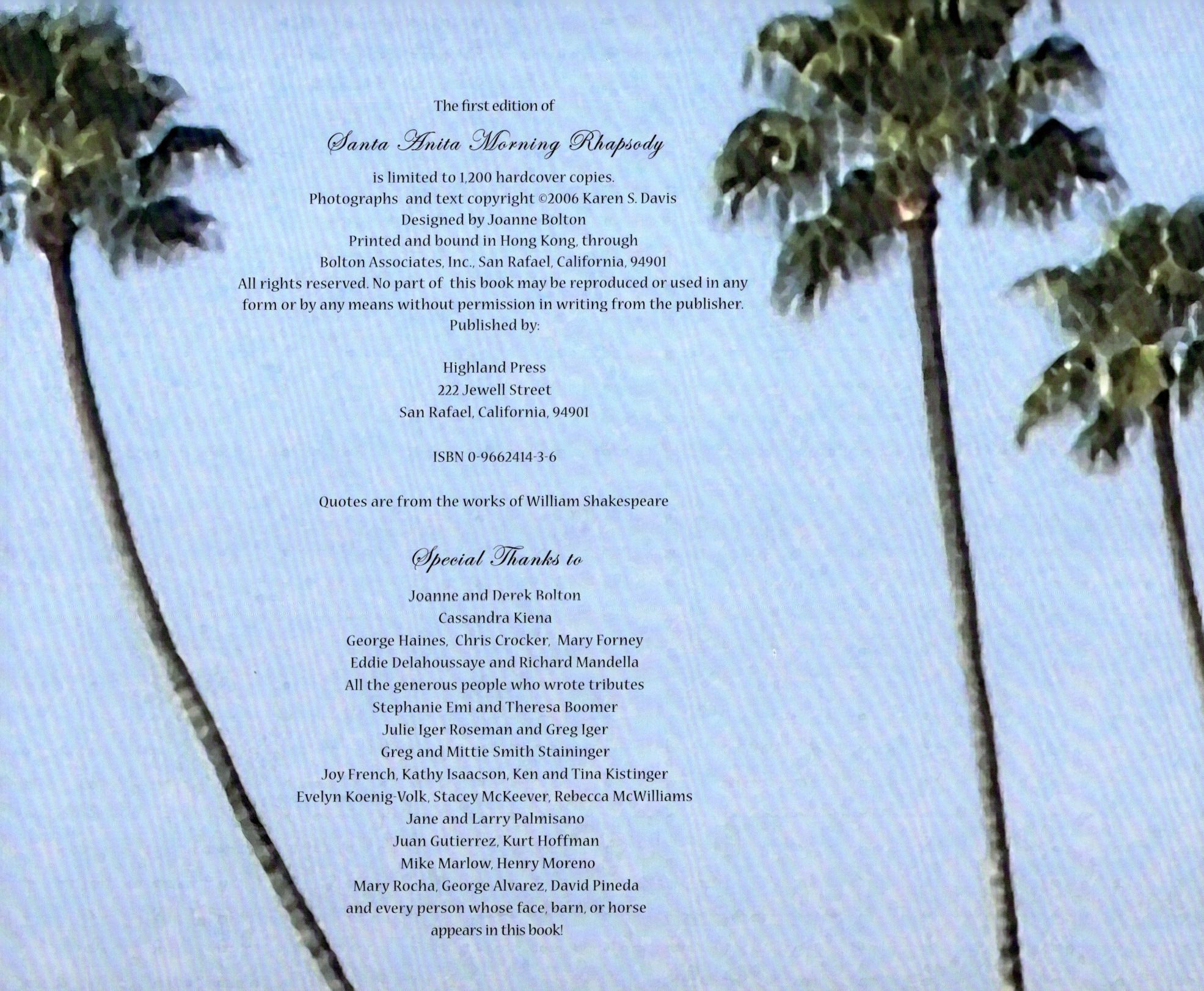

The first edition of

Santa Anita Morning Rhapsody

is limited to 1,200 hardcover copies.
Photographs and text copyright ©2006 Karen S. Davis
Designed by Joanne Bolton
Printed and bound in Hong Kong, through
Bolton Associates, Inc., San Rafael, California, 94901
All rights reserved. No part of this book may be reproduced or used in any
form or by any means without permission in writing from the publisher.
Published by:

Highland Press
222 Jewell Street
San Rafael, California, 94901

ISBN 0-9662414-3-6

Quotes are from the works of William Shakespeare

Special Thanks to

Joanne and Derek Bolton
Cassandra Kiena
George Haines, Chris Crocker, Mary Forney
Eddie Delahoussaye and Richard Mandella
All the generous people who wrote tributes
Stephanie Emi and Theresa Boomer
Julie Iger Roseman and Greg Iger
Greg and Mittie Smith Staininger
Joy French, Kathy Isaacson, Ken and Tina Kistinger
Evelyn Koenig-Volk, Stacey McKeever, Rebecca McWilliams
Jane and Larry Palmisano
Juan Gutierrez, Kurt Hoffman
Mike Marlow, Henry Moreno
Mary Rocha, George Alvarez, David Pineda
and every person whose face, barn, or horse
appears in this book!